DON'T BUILD ROLLERSKATES FOR BIRDS

BY

BECKY LODGE
(BA HONS) CIM

Published by:
Little Kanga Ltd
Suite 107, 5 Charter House
Lord Montgomery Way
Portsmouth
PO1 2SN

First published in 2018
Copyright © Becky Lodge 2018

ISBN: 978-1-5272-1466-8

Note: The material contained in this book is set out in good faith for general guidance and no liability can be accepted for loss or expense incurred as a result of relying in particular circumstances on statements made in this book.

Produced by Biddles Books, King's Lynn, Norfolk PE32 1SF

Contents Page

About The Author

Becky Lodge is a degree and Chartered Institute of Marketing qualified sales and marketing consultant and Founder based in the UK

Born in inner city Leicester in 1971, she has had an accomplished international sales and marketing career spanning over a quarter of a century; rising through the ranks to become one of the most accomplished and recognised sales and marketing directors in her vertical markets of operation (engineering and technology).

Having worked with and for, some of the largest brand names in the world including Ferrari, Carlsberg and Disney, Becky ended her employed career (before starting her own company) in the radio broadcast software and engineering sectors.

Her company, Little Kanga Ltd, was founded in 2015 from her kitchen table on a shoestring budget.

In 2017, Becky was selected from thousands of applicants in the UK to become one of 'Sky News 100 Women' (#100Women). These women are part of a movement dedicated to bringing gender parity into every aspect of business globally. She is also a fierce advocate of STEAM (Science, Technology, Engineering, Arts and Maths) for girls in schools.

Becky and her co-founder Laura Kenward have supported and coached over 3,000 start-up and early stage business owners in the last 3 years through their support group, 'StartUp Disruptors', which is dedicated to improving the social and economic impact of small business owners across the UK.

Dedications

To my family, thank you for your patience and love.
It means everything to me to have you in my life.

To my husband, Dan

Thank you for believing in me and being everything that I aspire
to be each day.

You are simply the best human being I know.

Laura Kenward

You are my rock – words aren't enough. I couldn't and wouldn't
want to do any of it without you.

Mark Chivers

You are simply one of the best people I have ever known. Thank
you for all your support.

Peter and Alice Hooley

Without your support, I wouldn't be where I am now.

Mark Pembleton

Thank you for your kindness and support.

Donna Jones

From 'this girl' to 'that girl' – thank you for all that you do and
will continue to do for me. Keep disrupting.

Uber

Fred, Eugenie, Brittany, Harri and the team at Uber – you rock!

Martin Waters

You're a ginger legend (and I can say that as one ginger to another!)

The StartUp Disruptors

Thank you to each and every member of our community. You inspire me every day. Your success is humbling. Laura and I could only imagine the trouble that we started with 9 people in a pub in 2016.

#LinkyBrains

Thank you for showing me that truly being yourself is all that really matters.

You know who you are.

Sky News

Thank you for choosing me as one of your Sky News #100Women, I will continue to support the gender parity and inclusion agenda by your side.

Louise – thank you for including me.

The Old Customs House – Gunwharf Quays

Emil and team thank you for hosting us, as well as keeping us fed and watered.

Emma Paxton - www.imagistic.co.uk

Thank you for drawing the bird for the book cover, testament to your creative talent – thank you.

Other notable mentions and supporters:

Epic institutions/others who have supported me along the way

- University of Portsmouth
- Portsmouth City Council
- The people of Portsmouth
- Funding Circle
- Eastleigh Borough Council
- Everyone involved in 'Hampshire Meet The Buyer'
- Victoria Lofthouse
- All my past and future customers and suppliers

Introduction

I want to help you.

You may think that sounds trite, but it's true.

As I write this sentence, I have been in business for over two and a half years and I have made the most gargantuan mistakes and had the most terrific successes.

I want to share with you my knowledge on how to avoid the pitfalls of starting up and maximising your successes, so that you can run a great business.

It's not going to be one of those weighty business books that you have to plough through. This is more an anecdotal story of the process of my business starting up and moving along from day one. It contains some hints and tips for you in terms of a little bit of sales and marketing theory.

The one thing that I wanted to write was something honest.

An account of my journey as a female business owner (and yes it is a differing experience if you are a woman running your own business, even in 2018!).

It's great to meet you and thanks for taking the time to read this book, whoever you are and wherever you are on your start-up business journey. I hope that you may find some of the information relevant and useful in your start-up or early stage business process.

So who am I?

I suppose I better start with a little bit more about my background.

I am from a generation that is 'pre-tech'; we are called 'Gen X'. At the time of writing this, I am 46 years old.

There is an assumption today, that entrepreneurs are all young and thrusting 'tech' or 'app' businesses across the globe.

Starting with a 'lean start-up methodology'.

Got to be honest in year one that was just a bunch of words that I really didn't understand.

I was reading around entrepreneurship as a topic and didn't recognise anyone that looked like me.

There were lots of 'mumpreneur' support groups – so I'm not a Mum or a parent, where do I get support? If you're not a Mum could you even join?

Female Entrepreneur networks – an unmitigated disaster for me. I had spent all my corporate life talking to men on-site about bacon butties and binge-drinking, how would I cope with over the canape conversations?

Basically, I'm an unashamed middle-aged Waitrose shopper (and sometimes Aldi - I like a bargain!) based in Portsmouth, Hampshire, UK.

There are thousands of women in the UK who are over 40 and now the 'lost Sex and the City generation'.

The generation that were told we could 'have it all' in the 1980's. Career; kids; promotion; marriage. The world was ours for the taking.

My name is Becky Lodge.

Many start-up business owners (in the UK), at the time of writing, are over 40 years old and this is indeed a very underestimated market.

Many people in 'middle age' will now be working longer. We are living longer and at this age, we are starting our businesses as an alternative to the working life and career that we have already experienced.

This time, we have knowledge and experience on our side.

Whilst media and advertising, and to some extent business, endlessly focus on the 'next generation and youth', what happens when you are over forty?

Do you know what? It doesn't really matter in business what age you are, the market decides who wins and who loses.

No matter who and how old you are doesn't matter, it's the business idea and execution of that idea that will ultimately dictate your future success.

So, this book is really for you (no matter what your age or where you shop!) to let you know that businesses come in all shapes and sizes and niches.

Owners are young and old and come from varying backgrounds, but the challenges in setting up a business are the same.

As I write this, around 80 new businesses an hour in the UK are being registered, so I know that you are out there (and hopefully, in you finding this book, I have reached you – Hello!).

I grew up and went to school in England and learned to write in both pencil and fountain pen (yes, real life ink!) Throughout my university education, I only used an electric typewriter, and that was only in my final year, to type my dissertation!

Cue shock and horror of anyone reading this who is younger than 35 years of age.

My typewriter was considered very 'cutting edge' in 1992,

as it had a Tipp-Ex function so that you could go back and overwrite your errors.

This technological shift is pivotal to you (dear reader) to understand, in terms of where I am in my life, and how this may differ to your experiences in life, if you are, for example, in your 20s or in your 60s. This book is a subjective viewpoint with some facts and theory and advice mixed in.

It's meant less as a teaching manual, simply more my view and story of how things began for me; basically my story. What I feel could be important advice for you, by sharing some of my knowledge and errors of judgement along the way!

So what else do you need to know about me before we get started?

Who is Becky Lodge?

I run a service-led business and am a qualified sales and marketing consultant. I studied at degree level and have a qualification from the Chartered Institute of Marketing (CIM). I am a guest lecturer in Sales at the University of Portsmouth, and for the majority of my employed career (before starting up my own business) I was employed in sales (business development) at director level.

I have always worked hard and enjoyed learning.

I don't think I am the most talented or naturally gifted person, but I have always put in more hours than anyone else. That's how you become successful; you keep practicing at it and out-work everyone to get to where you want to be.

My grandmother taught me very early on that to practice at the piano was the only way to improve.

I didn't really want to hear that at age 7, as I wanted to play in the garden with the rest of the kids, but discipline pays dividends and those lessons that your family teach you very early on are setting you up for success or failure later on in life.

So, what have I practiced at for the last 25 years?

Sales. I'm addicted to becoming better, learning and improving about all things selling. It's an art.

So why did I write this book for you?

I got fed up.

I got fed up of so much stuff in the market that simply glorifies an image for most start-up owners that is a 'fantasy'.

I want to 'bust some myths'.

This book is for you, wherever you are at, whatever you need and however I can help you (maybe just a little bit) in starting or growing your business.

One of the biggest issues when you start a business is being socially isolated, being alone tapping away on a laptop, stuck in the back bedroom swearing at Microsoft as it updates (again).

One of my habits (or addictions!) is to use social media to better connect with other like-minded small business owners.

Social media is a great way to engage with people across the globe and it has no geographic barriers. So, Bob in New York or Kiki in Sydney can chat with you 24/7/365, meaning you can share start-up stories and information in a way that was unimaginable when I started my career over 25 years ago.

I also post useful resources for pre-start-up businesses (those in the 'ideas phase') online including sharing the best start-up resources from around the globe.

I got so fed up with having to trawl all the information on all platforms; I now provide the support to help you on your journey as a start-up business owner.

So, that about covers the introduction. As we all know, entrepreneurs have a short attention span, so let's move on to the good stuff.

What else do you need to know right now?

I also co-founded a start-up support group called 'StartUp Disruptors'. You can find us on the following platforms – have a look.

Website: www.start-up-disruptors.co.uk

Instagram: www.instagram.com/startupdisruptors

Facebook: www.facebook.com/startupdisruptors

Twitter: www.twitter.com/solentdisruptor

I love technological change and progress. In marketing terms, I am an early adopter. That, in itself, as a woman, makes me somewhat unusual.

Early adoption simply means that I adopt ideas early or come up with ideas in advance of others, and I am not afraid of taking calculated risks. The majority of the population are late adopters (they wait for others to validate a product or service – they are more risk averse.)

You can read more on early and late adoption in books online, and without getting too technical, it forms a significant part of marketing theory, which is key to knowing your customer and markets.

(Search: Everett M Rogers – Diffusion of Innovations for more online.)

What You Need To Know About Setting Up Your Own Business

Being a 40+ female, living in the UK, surely makes me an unlikely candidate for 'entrepreneurship'.

What a great word. Entrepreneurship.

How glamourous and fashionable it sounds.

It conjures up thoughts of creative 'twenty-somethings' in loft-style apartments in New York, coming up with the latest tech app and getting a billion dollar investment.

Even Google started somewhere. In a garage you know.

The Oxford English Dictionary defines entrepreneurship as:

"A person who sets up a business or businesses, taking on financial risks in the hope of a profit."

So, for me, is it even the right word to apply?

Am I an entrepreneur, a start-up business owner, a freelancer or a combination of all of these terms?

Perhaps I should call myself an 'entre-start-lancer' or ESL?

Personally, I don't think the terminology really matters (but I am sure that someone will disagree with me here – and it wouldn't be the first time!).

I primarily wrote this book, as when I started in 2015, there was very little to help start-ups to prosper in the local area.

The UK government had withdrawn a lot of funding for business support and having sought advice from the 'usual' sources that were recommended, I found them to be too slow-moving with little knowledge of how technology could impact and create a start-up business, as well as the 'experts' understanding how pivotal social media is now.

Every 'advisor' had their hand out, but the 'advice' was outdated and inflexible. It didn't seem that anyone really understood what I was 'getting at'. I didn't want to borrow a sh*t load of money and put myself into debt, until I could prove that I had a business model that even worked, let alone customers that would want to pay for my services.

So the first question I wanted the answer to was:

'In reality, what does running your own business look like?'

The answer for me was:

For the first year (at least), I sat in my pyjamas a lot of the time crying at the kitchen table, alone at least three times a week. Because I was frustrated with everything and anything. It all seemed massively overwhelming. The dog was great company, but the conversations were limited.

My biggest cock-up was not having a non-disclosure agreement in place with a supplier, who then very sneakily managed to re-focus the customer on his role in the company, meaning that I lost out to the tune of £12,000 worth of ongoing retained business.

I trusted him, I shouldn't have done. I learned something here!

Note to self: Contracts are important.

This, however, was one of my darkest hours in year one. It almost finished me.

For six weeks it was all I could think about. I wasn't sleeping. I couldn't think about anything else.

It was my wonderful husband that simply said this to me:

"You have to remember why you started. The alternative is going back and getting a job, and I know that you don't want that."

That one sentence provided the focus that I needed to carry on.

I also went to see my last boss (to be honest for a bit of reassurance), he's a self-made man running a £5m company and I asked him:

"Did you ever get scared?"

(You have to understand the irony of me asking a gruff, matter-of-fact engineer in his late fifties this question and he simply said this):

"Becky if you are looking in the rear-view mirror you're not looking at the road ahead." He was absolutely right.

I keep this saying close at hand and look at it when I hit the inevitable self-doubt that we all have to overcome from time to time.

When I fail, I now recover in a split second and move on to the next thing that can immediately make a difference to moving things forward for the business.

But you may be sitting there not even having started your business yet, or you could be in the very early stages of doing so. So, my advice to you is this:

Start small with a few things that you can do and are pivotal to your very early stage success.

These are all based around the ability to ORGANISE your SYSTEMS and PROCESSES to support the basic day-to-day running of your business online and getting the basics in place for the tax department.

The top 5 small things that I urge you to get right from day one are as follows with regard to simple 'rookie' errors to avoid:

Don't use a Yahoo or Gmail e-mail address – the world has moved on; invest in getting your e-mail hosted by someone reliable and local to you fast.

Millennials with an enhanced level of tech knowledge will use other methods, but if you are over 40 years of age, with limited tech knowledge, then I found it easier to pay someone else.

Get the right accountant – one who can grow with your company, NOT just the cheapest.

I got let down early on and it cost me more money. I should have invested more time and money researching this area.

Don't get hung up on having a website – Facebook, Weebly and Wix provide a combination of cost-effective solutions for you.

Getting one of these set up, with your terms and conditions and having a non-disclosure agreement, are MUCH more important for you.

Yes, they cost money, but you need to be protected. Don't start spending ANY money on marketing until you are INSURED.

This scared the hell out of me recently when I asked a supplier to help me and they didn't have insurance!

Needless to say, I found someone fast that did.

Start talking to people - let them know that you are starting your business, look for those people that may be able to help you get some sales in through referral or help you resell.

Ideally, have some customers BEFORE you set up, as that's an indicator that people will BUY!

Get over yourself – nobody will even know that you have started a business, let alone care.

You aren't running a massive global corporation (yet) and being confident is one thing, coming over as a total a*sehole is another, so dial down the ego. It's not about you, it's about the customer.

The aim of the game when you start (especially if you don't have a lot of investment), is to acquire profitable customers cheaply and as quickly as possible, then retain them.

Top Tip: As soon as you get money back into the business and have profit, outsource the admin functions and low-level activity such as blogging and social media campaign management.

You are a business owner and need to concentrate on revenue-generating activities.

Why are you behaving as if you are an employee?

If you are not looking to build an empire (for example, you want a lifestyle business) then it may be OK for you to try and 'do it all', but you will only suffocate your growth by trying to do so. To build a £100k a year home-based business from nothing takes hard work and time.

Moving on…

I do have to chuckle when I read about 'entrepreneurship' on social media, especially articles that 'glamourise' the process.

Authors selectively miss out the bits about how hard you have to work to get known, here are some of my alternative titles for articles in the press or on social media that describe the fabulous journey of setting up your own business (meant with humour – obviously):

- "How to explain to your spouse that you won't be home on time (again)." – a Handy Guide.

- "Our 'top five tips' on how to avoid your bank manager."

- "Sales Prospects and Customers – why they never return your calls."

- "Credit Control – why the invoice is only the start."

I think that you get my drift...

This is why I am writing this first little book.

To hopefully help people like you who at this point may say, 'so far this all sounds familiar' or 'thank f**k, I thought that it was just me!'

The book is really to say to you, 'here is a warts and all account of my journey so far' (another new phrase coined by reality TV) and hopefully, it will give you some helpful hints and tips to help you build your own successful enterprise.

Year two was much harder for me than year one, and the emotional impact of running a business can only be described as being 'very interesting'.

So, what does the first year look like?

In your first year, you are full of enthusiasm and that drives you forward.

You're flushed with momentum at the shiny new business that you own.

You concentrate on mastering Canva and Instagram, and joining lots of Facebook support groups, thinking that this will bring in lots of sales.

You have lots of lovely business cards printed with a matching pull-up roller banner and consume lots of YouTube content from Tony Robbins and Gary Vaynerchuk.

By year two (especially if you don't have a co-founder), you can find yourself de-motivated and exhausted as the reality of business ownership has become apparent.

You realise the dog won't walk itself, the washing is piling up, the family are fed up of hearing about your 'next big project', and you spend most of the time answering e-mails in your pyjamas (after not getting dressed for three days in a row whilst pumping out another 12 hour day).

Suppliers are difficult to find and retain, nobody ever delivers what they say they will, you realise there's seasonality in your sales figures, and have no money to cover the cash flow of the death knell that is August in the UK market.

CRAP!

You need to find exceptional reserves of energy to continue working long hours, for small returns, with massively fluctuating revenue month on month.

You second guess each decision that you make and that can lead to indecision and analysis paralysis. The pressure on your mental health can be gargantuan.

It's truly important that you have an understanding of how your 'brain is built' your emotional motivators and drivers, you need to understand your capacity. Not only in terms of workload, but your emotional and mental resilience as your journey starts out and continues.

So, what can help here?

Start With Self

So, before you begin, I would suggest what I call 'Start with Self'.

So, What About You? Who are you?

What are you wanting to achieve in starting your own business?

I hope that because you are reading this now, you have already had the 'idea' or that defining moment, where you thought:

"That's it, I have had enough of this job/person/boss/work colleague/thing not working."*

*delete as applicable.

Or you are fed up with watching YouTube videos about entrepreneurship from 'influencers' and want to get 'stuck in'.

I had myself, (until 2015) followed a pretty traditional career path since graduating from University with a Creative Arts degree.

It's one of those 'Mickey Mouse' qualifications that don't really count for much (according to some ex-work colleagues), although I have never thought of myself as a 'natural' academic.

I was the one always out having a drink down the pub, rather than cramming at the last minute to get a 'first'. Also, I don't think I have necessarily had what could be called a traditional work path.

So how did work begin for me?

When I was 15 years old, I asked my Dad for more pocket money; he said jokingly that I should get a job. So, I did. I went to the local Job Centre and looked at the job board (in the old days the Job Centre was a government-funded place where jobs were placed on boards on bits of card. The centres do still exist in the UK, but they are all pretty much automated.) I then approached the desk to find out more and they rang to arrange an interview for me.

I duly went to the Chinese restaurant at the allotted time for the interview and got the job. It was working Friday and Saturday nights from 5pm-12am for £2.50 an hour.

My Dad was quite horrified.

The fact was though, up until then, I had £5 a week pocket money as well as what I was earning. So very early on, I think that my entrepreneurial tendencies were there.

My poor old Dad.

That's the danger with me, like a heat-seeking missile, if you tell me to do something, I probably will. If you tell me NOT to do something, I am probably more motivated to find a way to do it.

I am problem solver, always have been. It's the function I perform in the family, the person 'that does' or 'gets it done'.

I have been working ever since I was 15 years old, and I cannot really stop working or over-thinking, or looking at everything around me as an opportunity to improve something.

That's the way that my brain operates, and I refer to this as 'the way that I am built'.

One of my bosses once said to me (in anger):

"Were you born saying the word WHY?"

I'm always trying to learn and make sense of people's motivation and that's why I ended up selling, as in terms of psychology there's not a better career to best understand a person's emotional motivation to buy things. Sometimes things they don't even want or need, but they feel they must HAVE.

Various jobs throughout my life have helped me pay for my education, including dishwashing, cleaning toilets in my university halls of residence (nice) during the summer 'holidays/vacation', and working in catering at the World Student Games to pay my way. I have always wanted to improve and work. I was never bank-rolled, but I have always had the most tremendous family support.

When other students were away in Europe during my teens (with their parents having a good time), I was earning my keep in various bars and restaurants around the UK.

From my point of view, I have never fitted the 'norm' for a woman, I have never really 'fitted in' or been a 'joiner'. I'm a really crap girl.

There; I said it.

But I love bringing people together.

If you have ever studied Myers-Briggs in business, I am an ENFJ. People person, believer in the transformational power of people and what they can achieve together.

I don't like shopping, am not into clothes and hate going around shopping malls (I tend to have multiples of the same items in different colours) and I don't really like paying for anything that I can trade/barter or swap.

I don't have children (it was never really 'a thing' for me) and I hate wasting time.

It's so precious and finite and to me, there's always something that needs to be done or something to be learned.

I have been called everything during the course of my career from 'bullish' and 'overbearing' and 'totally unmanageable' to 'enthusiastic', a 'jack in the box' and 'utterly focussed and tenacious'.

I often challenge these perceptions, as I don't think that labels for women are useful and language can be very destructive.

Acceptance of yourself and others as they are is important and pivotal to who I am.

I'm just me. Like you are 'just you'.

Yet I still feel the drive to improve upon everything and anything. Just that little bit more...

I live for working and solving problems. I don't really care about money and I think that others care about it too much.

Money comes, it goes, and it sometimes makes good people do terrible things, or make bad decisions. You will have it. You will spend it. You will sometimes save it. You will sometimes spend it, foolishly.

But you will still be you, whatever state your finances are in.

My view is this, simply living a life to pursue money is not really a life. But then it takes all sorts to make the world turn. We are all different and that is what makes life and business exciting.

Where were we? (See, off again...oh yes, being a 'paid employee'/worker bee) ...

During my quarter century of employment, I was a worker through and through.

I was always the first in and last to leave; always the person working and worrying as if my life depended on it.

When most people looked aghast at extra work, I was the one asking for it.

In business, although very successful in all my employed roles, as a professional woman, I have been described as 'pushy' (ambitious), too direct (I still have no idea what that really means – results orientated?) and have also had managers that simply just didn't 'get me', or what I was really capable of doing for them.

I haven't had an easy career. Sales is a massively male-dominated environment, so you learn very fast to look after yourself. I am sure that there would have perhaps been easier choices, but then I would probably have been bored; I love a challenge.

I was such an early adopter in terms of everything that I saw in part of each new job role that made others uncomfortable.

What was screamingly obvious in terms of improvement to me often scared or intimidated others, who perhaps weren't as 'open' to ideas and certainly there are people that don't like change in life in the way that I actively embrace it.

So that's why I started up on my own.

But there was something that came before that, this influenced me greatly in my decision making and attitude towards my career and future start-up business path.

During 2008 both my husband and I were made redundant within 3 months of one another.

I lost my job and with it went my self-esteem.

I was devastated.

I went to work in a call centre to pay the bills and gradually worked hard to get back to full time work.

But it took its toll. I couldn't really function for a while.

At the same time, one of my friends lost her baby in childbirth. That put things in perspective. She was totally bereft, and I didn't know how to comfort her.

Some time passed. I worked on getting myself 'back in the game', but it was seemingly impossible. It was one of the toughest life lessons that I ever learned.

I went out for interviews and kept getting turned down.

Again, and again and again. Failure after failure. Rejection after rejection.

I went for over 100 interviews.

Jobs that I had easily been qualified for and would have got in the past were nowhere to be seen.

The excuses for not hiring me got more bizarre, I was 'too overqualified' or 'not quite the right fit'.

It was still the recession, and nobody was hiring. So, I kept working at the call centre to make ends meet.

One day I got a call from a recruitment agency, a local company was hiring, and they asked if I would go for an interview, they had a vacancy in sales and would like to put me forward for the role.

This company was well run, family-owned and ambitious, and willing to offer me the job after the interview went really well. It felt like a great fit.

This job showed me the power of teamwork, as well as the difference that a great company owner can make to the mental health and wellbeing of its staff.

It showed me the power of self-belief and choosing the right people for the right jobs.

I watched and learned from one of the greatest bosses I have ever had.

What he said, how he behaved, how he treated his staff and suppliers.

I had the best job ever and had been there nearly two years.

It was then, that I decided to leave employment and working for somebody else for good.

Was that ungrateful or an epiphany?

A great job. Fab boss. Good salary.

WHAT WAS I THINKING!

So why did I leave?

I was sitting in the office one day it was a day like any other. I was working through a pile of e-mails. I looked out of the window and had my 'defining moment'; that nagging voice in my head said, 'it's now or never sunshine!'

I simply didn't want to be looking back on my life at 85 years of age and thinking 'if only I'd had a go at having my own business', so I handed in my notice that day.

You can imagine the sheer delight of my husband when I told him this. But like the epic human being he was (and is!) he supported me in the decision.

I just wanted something different, after the years of continuously hitting massive sales targets and living each day on a 'knife edge' that most people would find both terrifying and immensely challenging.

I don't know why sales and I as a career pairing have worked.

It's a combination of wanting to always learn and spend time with people. I have sold pretty much everything over the course of my career. From cars (my first job role straight out of university in 1993), to corporate workwear and cigarettes (forgive me, I was young and thought it was a good idea) to generators and radio broadcast software.

I am the ultimate polymath.

From telesales to account management and business development, I have spent the last 24 years (before starting up) learning how to sell, influence, negotiate, build sales pipelines and close the deal.

So, I should be pretty well qualified to run my own business, right?

WRONG.

There's so much to learn, it's a whole new world.

Here's how I break it down for people that are new to the world of start-up.

It's important that you can understand the phases.

Pre-Start-Up – The Ideas Phase

This is where you have a great idea but haven't yet started trading or gained any customers. Some call this the 'pre-start-up' phase.

There are so many ideas in your head that the options are never-ending.

But you need to start to 'sift', to see which ones are worth thinking about, then act upon them and take them a little further to investigate and validate your idea(s) further.

Start looking at the business model canvas to get your ideas down and out of your busy brain.

In this phase, you also need to talk to your friends and family about the reality of starting your business, and how that will impact on them.

The following are the realities of running your own business:

Friends and family – What they and you need to know

- You need to be honest with them; if you are to see this through, it will affect all that you do.

- Your time won't belong to them anymore.

- You will have no social life.

- You will always be working or thinking about work, even in the middle of the night when you are wide awake.

- You will have no weekends at all and you may not sleep a lot.

- You will miss out on family events and evenings out. That is what this will take in terms of your commitment to succeed.

- There is no easy way.

- It will put your closest relationships to the test; it may break your marriage or closest partnerships.

- You need to think that your 'big idea' will be worth the above.

- It is not for everyone.

- If you are prone to having ideas and then not following them through, then don't start your own business or if you do, find a co-founder who can execute the parts that you cannot.

- You cannot just get a team to run things for you, you need to lead. You need a mission and you need to drive it. Every day of the year, for the rest of your life.

- Are you ready to make that choice yet?

- Are your family and friends ready?

- Are you mentally ready?

- Are you resilient enough?

- Can you be told 'no' each and every day, all the time and still remain upbeat and forward-thinking, even when you have been up for twelve to fourteen hours straight?

- This is not about macho culture; this is about the will to do what it takes to succeed.

- You may be earning nothing or £3 an hour in the early stages. For a very long time.

- Are you prepared to make sacrifices?

- How will this impact you emotionally and psychologically?

- How do you deal with stress?

- Day in and day out, for the rest of your life? Even when your kids are growing up?

During this ideas stage, I would suggest that you undertake multiple psychometric and personality tests. These are commonly used in the recruitment and selection of sales teams. It identifies your personality traits and how you like to be managed.

In the world of start-up, I cannot understand when articles say, 'know yourself', that what they actually should say is 'take a psychometric test', and then take a long hard look in the mirror and be honest with yourself.

You will always be learning at such an accelerated rate when you start. This 'pre-start-up' time should be spent wisely. The more you know about yourself, the more competitive advantage you will have in the market, when you later launch your business.

When you come up against a barrier or problem in your business, you can then step back and look at the issue more objectively, as you will know more about what drives and motivates you, what skill-set you have and what skills you need to compensate for/develop.

You can go back and refer to the tests and profiles and think, 'right, that's how I react, and this is how I get over it, fast!'

There are plenty of free tests online, find out what drives you; find out what you are no good at. Yes, we all have things that we cannot do, and this can go against the usual bullish entrepreneurial ego, but you need to know yourself first.

I call this process: 'Start With Self'.

Find out what motivates you and bores you rigid. For me, I am driven by being with people and getting results (back to Myers-Briggs ENFJ).

But you would never employ me as your accountant. It would be commercial suicide.

I know this as a fact. I know myself. Find out how you will emotionally react to situations, are you quick to anger?

Do you procrastinate?

Are you an introvert or extrovert?

What other personalities and people do you need as your business grows to compensate for the parts that you are weak at?

You need to know your strengths and weaknesses; you need to be brutally honest with yourself and those around you.

This may take the form of sitting down with all your close friends and family and discussing the impact, right down to who will do the shopping, put the kids to bed and take the dog for a walk.

You may not be able to do any of these things, for a long, long time.

Tip: Know yourself - 'Start With Self'.

Your start-up will test you to your limits (like a bad relationship) so do all that you can, in advance, to prepare and keep reading and learning.

You never stop.

You're 'all in'.

Become a sponge. For every. Little. Detail.

Why People Matter

How is running your own business different?

The one thing that is true across all of the job roles that I have ever had in sales is the seemingly obvious.

You need the 'punters'/customers to sell to, otherwise, you don't have a business.

They need to be ready to buy, they have to know who you are before they buy from you, and you need to be obsessed from day one of opening the doors in acquiring and nurturing your customers to stay with you and buy more.

You are also (most of the time), in a massively congested, mature market with established competitors with loads of marketing budget. Highly primed sales teams and experienced business owners, who will do all that they can from day one to get you to, at the very least, 'go away' or, at the very best, 'shut up shop' as fast as possible.

Without people, there is no business. No customers. No transactions. No competitors.

Without a customer having a 'need', there is no product or service to sell to meet that 'need', there would be no 'market'.

So, we need to talk about the people.

Who they are, how they influence all that you do in business, and why, as an entrepreneur, you need to think about what people you need to support your business from day one.

Oh, and leave the 'build it and they will come' mentality (if you have it - along with the end of this sentence). Know yourself and don't delude yourself. You have competition, a lot of it. They shout louder, undercut you, have larger marketing and sales budgets, and they will use them against you. That's business.

That will be one of the best pieces of advice that you will get before you have wasted thousands of pounds/dollars finding out first-hand that people don't care about you, as they don't even know who you are yet.

Planning the 'People'

From day one of your business, you will come into contact with others. People are unpredictable, they are human beings.

People and business owners who are natural introverts may really struggle with this concept.

As an ambivert, I need the introverts, they are amazing at finishing stuff, detail-orientated champions, but like the wicked witch in the Wizard of Oz, they are more likely to want to melt through the floor than go and sell something. Unfortunately for introverts there is no system, marketing technique or other tech solution, that replaces relationships with others and how we can influence and 'read' people when face-to-face. That's why co-founded businesses with opposing personality types often thrive, as they balance out each other's weaknesses.

Most people will oppose every single idea that you have when you start up (often with good reason – they often know more than you!). You are going to need a lot of help (and fast) at the start.

Even more imperative, is the fact that you are going to need unshakeable self-belief, and money in the bank, to get you through the first few years (or a spare room with someone who pays for everything!).

It goes without saying that you should speak to your family and friends before you start out. Many articles also say, start your business on the side of another job. They are all right. You should. If you are sensible and have common sense.

I didn't. I gave up my job and just 'had a go at it'.

People I told along the way were sometimes shocked, but I thought (again from my point of view) 'what is the worst that can happen? I fail, I'll go back and get another job'. Both arrogant and stupid I suppose, especially when you have bills to pay.

But having been made redundant in my employed career, three times in twenty odd years, I thought that I was better off being in control of my own destiny.

Besides, technology has changed everything. This I viewed as being a great opportunity in a global market. Opportunities and money abound now. Interest rates in the UK have never been lower (2016) and Brexit has changed the UK political landscape to allow more disruption in the business landscape than ever before.

But most people are fearful and risk averse. They have dependants and credit card bills and responsibilities and, as adults, hopefully some common sense.

For the first time in 2015, I realised that I had marketable skills that can be sold from and to anywhere. My home could be an office. There was free advertising (social media channels), no need for premises, landlines and infrastructure (like in the old days). The cost of operation has lowered for service-led businesses across the world. That was an amazing sense of freedom.

But anyway, I have wandered off the point (I am prone to that when I feel passionate about something, so watch out for more of this) so where was I, oh yes, the people.

For the purposes of this book and for you to get the best from it, I can only talk about a service-led, business-to-business (B2B) offer, or my market of operation and again, I can only talk about this in relation to where my business is at the moment. This changes daily.

I see the following observations, as being outside your business plan (although a total pain in my eyes, business plans are easier to write; this factors in things like time to sort out in everyday terms and how much this impacts on your day-to-day time and planning; which you sometimes don't see as a cost, but actually is!), the irony is though, that business plans are really for larger business models and traditional business operations. So, try using something instead called the 'business model canvas' which is a one page business plan.

There is little (as Eric Ries noted in his book 'Lean Startup'), that applies to the acceleration and exponential growth that all successful start-ups should have in terms of 'old style' business planning.

But the banks, accountants and financial institutions are still insisting on implementing old style paperwork and practices, that simply may not work for a pre-start-up business owner who is 'bootstrapping' a business and taking profit and investing it straight back into the business.

(NB. Bootstrapping means building your business with little or no money and putting all the profits back into the business to continue to build it).

Why your network matters

If you have not got a strong business and friendship network, this is the area to start working on as early as possible. Again, the 'people' cannot be underestimated here.

This is because a great deal of your revenue in the early years will come from leveraging your existing connections and social networks. PAY ATTENTION HERE. Because, as the saying goes, 'your network is your net worth'.

If you have a small circle of friends and acquaintances, start to extend it. You need to talk to as many people as possible and get to know them. These people ARE your potential CUSTOMERS when you start your company, so invest the time to get to know more people and local influencers in your home area.

An 'influencer' can be a local MP, group organiser, leader, business leader, anyone that has a large group or following can be useful to you, as they have the 'audience' and influence over that audience to help you and your business grow. This is before your brand starts to gain traction, and also because people still (in the UK), buy from people they know, like and trust.

When people want to find a company to use, they ask their direct network. Facebook has recently introduced a feature called 'recommendations' and this is a prime example of people being able to ask their friends on Facebook to recommend a company or service to them. In the 'old days' it used to be a referral at work over a coffee, or 'down the pub', but now social media is used extensively for referrals. For business, the number one platform (for business-to-business) is Linked In.

Customers will research you and your business through social media, looking at customer testimonials (this is called 'social proof'), to check out that you are trustworthy and competent. It's important that you have a presence, but you may not be able to afford to do it all at once.

There is a sales myth here that needs busting.

If you met someone today, in B2B even if they are ready to buy your service, it will still take you 7-12 contacts with that potential customer (prospect) to convert them to a sale. What we mean by contacts are: e-mails, phone calls, meetings, etc. I do a great deal of training around sales processes and attendees are always shocked that it takes so long from first contact to convert a customer to buy.

Also, you won't sell to everyone you meet. So that's why you need a large VOLUME in terms of a potential audience to sell to.

The other thing is that, statistically, even then, you may not convert them if you do not have the skills that it takes to do so.

Why do your existing network and contacts matter?

Primarily, for collaborative working purposes are there other companies that will resell your product or service for you during the early stages, and for supply chain purposes, what and who will you need to get started?

By reselling, I mean they could sell your product/service to their customers and take a percentage of the profit from each sale. Great examples of this business model are companies like Avon. Even Amazon offers this service to smaller traders online.

Who & What Is A Customer?

Who can buy your product or service?

If you are selling a product directly to the consumer (Business to Consumer known as 'B2C') then every contact that you have **could** represent an opportunity for a sale (for example, if you are selling ice creams or socks, but don't try selling rollerskates for birds as it will never take off - sorry, couldn't resist it). But in reality, not everyone will want to buy your product or service. As a business owner, you may think that not having a 'niche' would give you more opportunity. In fact, the reverse is true.

You need to be very clear about who you are selling too. So much so that if you met them in the street, you could describe how they look, where they shop and what their interests are.

In marketing terms, we call this 'buyer personas'.

You may have more than one 'buyer persona' but all of your marketing and sales activity is targeted at these groups.

For example, if you are a manufacturer of soft drinks aimed at teenagers, you will not use the same marketing and advertising tactics as those who are selling to middle-aged Waitrose shoppers.

So, you need to get to know your ideal target audience of buyers as fast as possible and the way to do this is market research.

This strikes fear into the hearts of a lot of new business owners, but it shouldn't. The more that you know your customer, the more you can ultimately solve their problems and sell more to them.

Some simple market research techniques may be: taking 10 questions on a sheet of A4 when you go to networking events and asking people to help you by answering them.

Questions should be simple, for example:

- Would you buy this product or service?

- What age are you? (You can provide multiple choice tick boxes!)

- Where do you live?

- What are your hobbies?

- Where do you shop?

- What do you do for a living?

- How much would you pay for this product or service?

- What do you like about the product/service?

- What information would you like to see about it and in what format?

- How would you like to buy this product/service (on-line/shop/face-to-face)?

Please note that if you are keeping people's personal data, then you need to follow the regulations and have the necessary consents for data protection. You can check out the following website or the information on the Information Commissioner's Office website (UK). https://ico.org.uk/

Note: In the UK you need to be GDPR compliant and information on this is available on the above website.

This simple market research system can help you build a picture of what your ideal target audience looks like and what they will buy and at what price they will buy it at.

If all the feedback is negative, then you know that you have to change or 'pivot' your offer. It is better to know at this stage, than when you have launched and invested thousands in your business.

Business owners really underestimate this phase. So many that I have personally advised, get wrapped up in promoting themselves and the business, before they have even established whether there is actually a market that needs servicing or, in fact, whether there is even a problem that needs solving.

You can conduct this kind of research anywhere, at the bus stop, waiting for a cab, in the high street on a Saturday. Just ask people what they think. Don't forget to give them your details or business card in case they later want to buy from you!

Local Brand Awareness

Aim to get known as fast and as early as you can in your local 'home' area. Use as many tech tools as possible, such as social media to accelerate your local presence and 'get your name out there'.

Try and do one platform really well. Don't be afraid to do things that others may not do.

You are not memorable if you perpetuate the status quo. A strange thing will also happen. You will gain followers or people really won't like you. You cannot please everyone, so don't try to. Not everyone will buy from you, but they are more likely to buy from you if you explain to them WHY you started and what your VISION is.

Use social media platforms to 'explain why' you started up. For my business, I use LinkedIn and Twitter. This is because I sell business-to-business. Also, you don't have enough hours in the day to get it all done. I try and post daily on all channels and use video as much as possible as it gets more attention and 'traction' online.

Even if you work 12 hours a day, five days a week, that's still only 60 hours and you need to apportion your time to the activities that bring you the most money and attention.

Why Sales Is The Only Focus

When you start a business, there's a pretty rudimentary process that you need to get to grips with.

Money in vs money out.

Sales is all that matters and sales cures all for the new start-up business owner.

You need some income and normally FAST!

In a service based business-to-business world, to sell to people you need to quote, to quote you need to meet people, and to meet people, you need to get dressed and go out and network. Door knock, get referrals from friends, and ask existing customers for recommendations.

Now, the social sellers will say 'door knocking' it's ancient and outdated.

I use the term here to cover virtually 'door knocking' online too via social media.

You need to contact people in order to sell to them.

Unless you have an online shop.

But then you need to apply the same principles to your inbound sales and marketing strategy and techniques too.

You still need to contact people, and then you need a lot of people (volume) to want to buy from you.

So, take some action!

Go and tell people what you do, host free workshops and speak to local interest groups, do talks and lectures to get people talking about you.

Give your time freely as long as there is a tactical reason for doing so.

You need that free time to lead to a referral or an introduction, so that you can later turn it into a sale.

For example, when I started up, I did 2-3 'expert speaker' free workshops each week.

But, they were held in start-up hubs across the city, universities where I knew my ideal customers were hanging out. These may not be the 'traditional' chambers of commerce or networking events. Because I couldn't find local networking events that worked for me and my business, I eventually set up my own. This now attracts my ideal customer to me directly, and together we have built one of the most robust business networking groups, of which all attendees are now gaining business from it.

If you cannot find it, and there is at least one other person saying that they have the same problem as you that could be a business opportunity for you to tap in to.

Our online and offline networking group started with 9 people in a pub opposite Laura's flat (she's my long-suffering co-founder) and it has now grown to over 1000+ online members (check out the website at this address):

www.start-up-disruptors.co.uk

Why did we start the group?

Our 'WHY' for starting was that myself and my co-founder Laura, were fed up with hearing 'horror stories' of people being asked to pay extortionate charges (often up front) for services generally. People charging for stuff that people simply didn't need or want. To protect people from the charlatans in the start-up market.

There were, and still are, many!

So, we asked around and found out we were not alone. People started to share their experiences with us.

It all began in the pub. As lots of great things do!

Brand awareness is key to start-up success.

So, what's the key to successful awareness then?

In my opinion the key is getting known locally and almost imitating what politicians do during election time, going out, meeting and greeting, contacting the local press for coverage, it all adds up.

This activity will help with the brand awareness of your business.

I was sure in the early days of setting up that all the wonderful work that I was doing in my bright shiny new business, would be immediately identified and I would become known.

Everything (and I mean everything) takes a lot longer in business than you think! It's a marathon and not a sprint.

Market traction takes years. Like 5-10 years. So don't fall victim to the trap of over-optimism in expecting that you can somehow 'play the system' and win people over.

I will, however, be able to highlight some things below that will truly make a difference to your business very early on. Most people don't like to do them, as it makes them uncomfortable.

But in the very early stages of your business you ONLY need to become great at SELLING!

Top Tips:

Call people – pick up the phone and talk to them, ask their advice, find out about their business. Contact them via their social media feeds and show an interest in what they are doing. Ask how you can support them.

Meet people – talking brings benefits and sales. Go and knock on their door, don't wait to be asked for a meeting, it will never happen; ask a friend for an introduction and go to see them.

Spend time working out what your sales goals are each week – set yourself a target that scares you, speak to 5 people a day, cold call 5 people a day, door knock on a trading estate, meet 10 people at a networking event and then MEASURE the success from each of those activities.

As is stands today (after 25 years sales experience), these are the quickest wins:

Ask existing customers for referrals to people in their network that would buy from you - if you are not trading then ask your friends and family for referrals in the same way, then contact those people. Alternatively, you can use all your social media channels in the same way and put a 'call out' to your network, asking for referrals to others who are likely to buy.

Find local influencers - these are the people locally that are well known. The person that people are always talking about. They are an influencer. They will have access to a large network of people and often have a high profile in the local community.

You can tweet them or contact them through social media. Offer to do something for them, a free talk, workshop or learning session. GIVE FIRST.

One of the most fatal errors that I have seen from direct observation and feedback from my start-up comrades, is the fact that most start-up owners and entrepreneurs adopt the 'build it and they will come' mentality.

If there is one thing that I can tell you now; nobody cares that you are thinking about starting up, or that you have started up (with the exception of your close family).

That sounds brutal, but nobody knows that you are there <u>and they don't care.</u>

It is your job to make them aware and show them your unique selling point (USP) and differentiation (what you do better than anyone else and how). No matter if you are a freelancer or a multi-million pound tech start-up, your journey is the same. You are not unique.

It will be your responsibility to garner attention and desire to create a customer, as per the infamous Peter Drucker's famous words:

'The purpose of a business is to create and keep a customer.'

Stick the above quote on your fridge, phone, bedstead, office wall, bathroom mirror or your forehead.

If you cannot answer how you will make that happen before you start your business, you have a lot of work to do!

(NB: if you don't know who Peter Drucker is, then you have some reading to do immediately. Grab the Kindle/phone download or go old school and go to the library).

Identify Your 'Critter':
How To Manage Your Mindset

In order for you to win as a start-up business/small business owner, your mindset is key.

In my years of experience, there are only two motivating emotions that lead to a buying decision (or sales rejection) and these emotions are fear and love.

Emotions are the driver of us as humans

I wanted to share and write a little bit about fear in this book. As I believe that there are only two emotions that define our actions in life.

Fear and love.

But what has this got to do with your mindset?

Many of our decisions are fear based, because we are humans and it's the mechanism of 'fight or flight' that keeps us alive!

In business many people act from a place of fear.

That voice in your head that says the following:

'What will people think of me if I make a mistake?'

'How humiliating would that be?'

'What if I cannot do it?'

'How much money would that cost me?'

'What if things go wrong?'

'What if my competitor is at this event?'

These kinds of things pop into our heads when we are typically alone, bored or tired or unfocussed.

You need to 'train' your brain to ignore these thoughts. Then as and when they pop up, get them out of your brain as soon as you can. There are plenty of audio books online about mindset for business; start to read or listen to them.

I was having a conversation with someone recently and said to them that performance in business is exactly like sport.

Can you imagine a heavyweight boxing champion going into the ring expecting to lose?

It's not going to happen, as all their sports training and mindset is 'set' around winning.

The same is true in business, you need to learn to want to 'win'. If you don't, you won't get where you need to be.

Controlling your inner critic ('The Critter')

You will have to learn to control the negative self-talk and imposter syndrome; this time the voice is back saying 'what if someone finds out I'm no good?'

I call my inner critic 'The Critter' and he pops up from time to time and we have some interesting internal conversations, but he doesn't rule me anymore.

Get a piece of paper and draw your 'Critter'.

Typically, they are destructive; mayhem-seeking and massively negative.

In order to be a productive business owner, the best way to combat FEAR is through ACTION.

If you have no TIME to think, because you are too busy 'doing', then your mindset and business becomes more productive.

A career in sales taught me that. If you are on the phone all day, in meetings and then off to the gym or out with friends, the 'Critter' doesn't have time to creep up.

Think about all the really successful people that you know and admire for a moment.

You know who they are; you may want to write their name(s) below:

Name:

What do they do well?

What's their character like?

Why do people like them?

Chances are, they talk and move around a lot or are always active. Many are constant networkers and popular people that it is hard to get time with them because of that.

Do you know someone who is ALWAYS talking on their mobile phone? They're successful and always positive – right?

This is not a given but learned behaviour, we choose our emotions, we choose how we feel in the morning when we get up and go to work. Yes, of course as humans, we all have 'off' days and phases in our lives, but as a business owner, you need to minimise these times, as it will suffocate your business and growth process.

As well as your business, your mind needs to be in the right place.

So, what about LOVE?

Think about LOVE for a moment.

Kindness, giving without expectation, action for others (your children and family, for example).

Compassion and an overwhelming sense of belonging, the moment that you win a race at school, get praised or compliment someone.

Those are actions based on LOVE.

The point of this is....

You get to choose how you feel and how you react to circumstances and events.

Nobody controls your world – except you!

Should you act with FEAR or with LOVE in your business?

I find that acting with kindness, trying to forgive (even when I don't feel like it!) is much more empowering than trying to 'get even' or 'get one over' someone.

What's the point in that?

Generally, when you give something (without the expectation of receiving something in return), that has led me to a much better place in business.

Let's be clear here. I am not saying you shouldn't be heard or stand your ground if challenged.

What I am saying is that as an educated adult, I have a choice.

You have a choice.

So, choose wisely as it will affect your reputation in the market and your customers WILL find out. People talk all the time.

They ask around. The truth will out!

Don't let your 'Critter' rule your mindset or your business and if they do, then seek help and support from friends, family or your other start-up business connections locally, they will support you through your toughest business phases.

If it's something more serious then don't be afraid to ask for help. There's no shame in it and what matters most is that you are OK.

Useful books for your on-going start-up journey:

Positive Intelligence – Shirzad Chamine www.positiveintelligence.com

The 7 Habits Of Highly Effective People – Stephen R Covey

Both of these authors are recognised legends in their fields.

In Covey's book, he also covers task and time management, which are pivotal to the success of the entrepreneur journey that you are on.

Learning from others is truly important if you want to succeed.

There are also plenty of groups on Linked In that you can join around subject areas such as 'Start-up' and 'Entrepreneurship'.

These networks also represent opportunities to link globally with like-minded people that may become your suppliers and customers over time too, so keep an open mind.

Don't forget that you can also join our FREE closed Facebook group for support.

Like-minded people on the same journey, sharing successes and sometimes seeking solace if the week has been challenging:

www.facebook.com/startupdisruptors

Search for our group of the same name on Facebook and request to join it.

Some Final Words

I started out wanting to write a short-guide that you may find useful in your start-up business journey.

I hope that you have found it illuminating!

To conclude, the only thing that matters to me in business is keeping my mindset as focussed as possible on the end goal.

Goal setting is pivotal but Rome wasn't built in a day (and believe me I've tried!).

Motivating yourself is one of the biggest challenges that you have.

In the very early stages, you are not actually competing with external competitors in your business, you are mentally competing with yourself.

It's pivotal that you have the tools and support necessary to undertake this massive task.

It's also OK to fail, just fail quickly and learn from it.

Don't be defeated, try not to get upset (or try to limit the time that you are upset as it distracts you from your 'endgame').

Repeatable consistent successful actions are what win. Tenacity, persistence. These are learned behaviours that you can acquire.

So, what about the money?

Brand awareness building and sales growth go hand in hand, but you need MONEY to survive and grow, even if you are running a social enterprise or CIC.

The one thought I use every day is: 'how is this activity adding to the bottom line of the business or working towards bringing me more sales?'

A quick word about being asked to do things for free.

People will approach you and say, can you do this for free? It would be a great way to get 'your name out there'.

Here you need to exercise your own judgement.

For example, if it's a talk to your potential target audience of customers and you can follow up and convert them to sales, then great!

If it's not leading to a sale or a referral, or if time is short, you have to decide if you want to do it.

The same is true if you get asked for lots of free products as donations.

If they are offering free press coverage or sending out e-mails to potential customers with your logo on then you may say 'yes'; if it's for the local scouts, then you have to take a view (sometimes it's not always about selling if you are community minded!).

This doesn't mean doing everything for free, some things you may wish to do if you feel that later it will be beneficial for you, but don't feel obligated.

If you are a believer in 'gut instinct' then it is always right. No matter how much your head tries to rationalise, sometimes your intuition is just more accurate. Don't ignore it.

I hope that you have enjoyed my sharing with you some of my early stage start-up experiences during this short book and I am sure that in the fullness of time I may be encouraged to write another.

But in the meantime, I wish you all the best in your start-up endeavours and if I can help at any time, then please do not hesitate to ask.

Good luck with your onward start-up journey!

I look forward to seeing your own story in print very soon, if there is anything that I can help with, then please refer to the social media links at the start/end of this book, or link with me today on LinkedIn online, you can send me a message and let me know how you felt about the content of this book and if it helped you in any way, then please do let me know.

Here are some links (so that you can contact me):

If you would like to book me as an expert speaker too, then I would also be delighted to hear from you.

Contact me NOW:

Becky Lodge on LinkedIn:

https://uk.linkedin.com/in/beckylodge

Find me on Twitter

www.twitter.com/yourlittlekanga

Join our community TODAY!

StartUp Disruptors:

If you wish to join our start-up community so that we can help you with your business growth then you can subscribe here:

www.start-up-disruptors.co.uk/subscribe

Find us on Facebook:

www.facebook.com/startupdisruptors

Find us on Instagram:

www.instagram.com/startupdisruptors

Talk to us on Twitter #startupdisruptors

www.twitter.com/solentdisruptor

I look forward to hearing more from you about your start-up journey and successes soon.

Keep disrupting!